Homechild

Homechild

Joan MacLeod

Talonbooks

Talonbooks
P.O. Box 2076, Vancouver, British Columbia, Canada V6B 3S3
www.talonbooks.com

Typeset in New Baskerville and printed and bound in Canada.
Printed on 100% post-consumer recycled paper.

First Printing: 2008

The publisher gratefully acknowledges the financial support of the Canada Council for the Arts; the Government of Canada through the Book Publishing Industry Development Program; and the Province of British Columbia through the British Columbia Arts Council and the Book Publishing Tax Credit for our publishing activities.

Library and Archives Canada Cataloguing in Publication

MacLeod, Joan, 1954-
    Homechild / Joan MacLeod.

A play.
ISBN 978-0-88922-582-4

    1. Home children (Canadian immigrants)–Drama. I. Title.

PS8575.L4645H59 2008   C812'.54   C2008-901052-3

Homechild was first produced at CanStage (Canadian Stage Company) in the Bluma Appel Theatre in Toronto in January 2006 with the following:

ALISTAIR   Eric Peterson
FLORA   Patricia Hamilton
LORNA   Brenda Robins
EWAN   Tom Rooney
WESLEY   Randy Hughson
DORRIE   Joyce Campion
JEAN   Barbara Gordon
KATIE   Lara Jean Chorostecki

Director: Martha Henry
Set & Costume Designer: Astrid Janson
Lighting Designer: Paul Mathiesen
Original Music: Stephen Woodjetts
Stage Manager: Lauren Snell

This revised version of *Homechild* was produced at the Belfry Theatre in Victoria in September 2007 with the following:

ALISTAIR   John Krich
FLORA   Terry Tweed
LORNA   Jillian Fargey
EWAN   Craig March
WESLEY   Andrew Wheeler
DORRIE   Margaret Martin
JEAN   Donna White
KATIE   Jennifer Paterson

Director: Roy Surette
Set Designer: Pam Johnson
Costume Designer: Karen Levis
Lighting Designer: Gerald King
Stage Manager: Melissa Rood

Homechild was commissioned by CanStage in 2001 and in 2002 it was part of their Play Creation Group program. I am grateful to the playwrights who were part of that group. The writing of this play was also made possible with the assistance of the 2004 Banff PlayRites Colony—a partnership between the Canada Council for the Arts and Alberta Theatre Projects. I am also indebted to Martha Henry, Marty Bragg and to Bonnie Green for helping bring this project to fruition. I would like to also thank the workshop actors at both CanStage and Banff as well as the actors from both the first and second production who brought much to the development of this script. I want to thank also my friends Shelagh Kareda, Don Hannah, Ken Garnhum, Morris Panych, Roy Surette, Ninette Kelley and Bill Gaston. Thank you as well to the University of Waterloo for their terrific web site on home children. Kenneth Bagnell's book *The Little Immigrants* was an invaluable source of both information and inspiration. My family, once again, graciously let me go and fly across the country too many times, often for much longer than they wanted. Thank you. Finally thank you Iris Turcott for your insight, wisdom and friendship.

This play is in memory of my parents Muriel MacLeod (MacMillan) and Fred MacLeod—born and raised on farms a few miles apart in Glengarry County.

Cast

ALISTAIR	late eighties
EWAN	Alistair's son, fifty
LORNA	Alistair's daughter, mid forties
FLORA	Alistair's sister-in-law, late seventies
WESLEY	neighbour, fifty
DORRIE	Wesley's mother, late eighties
KATIE	Alistair's sister, six
JEAN	Alistair's sister, eighty

The play takes place in summer and fall 1999 in Glengarry County in eastern Ontario. Most of the action is in and around Alistair's house which is rundown and old with hayfields, dirt and trees all around. It is no longer a working farm just as Alistair is no longer a working farmer.

Katie lives in another reality.

Prologue

KATIE wades through the hayfield.

KATIE

Jackie and me, we come to Kingskettle on the train. Way
there in the country. Fields and rock and sheep.
Whoosh ... goes the train. *Whoosh* goes Jackie. *That's a
cow having a piss.* Jackie says that to make me laugh. He
don't know cows. 'Til now we don't know nothing but
Edinburgh.

The widow in Kingskettle, Mrs. Parsons, the one who
took us in, she's fat. She makes biscuits on Saturday
afternoon. *Her arse is bigger than sixteen Katies.* Jackie says
that to make me laugh.

We sleep in a room out back there. The garden, you
see it through the slats. You see black sky and the clouds
in slivers. The wind comes too. *Bundle me up Jackie.* He
wraps me up in the blanket and piles up clothes for his
self. *Bundle me up, bundle me up.* Jackie holds me tight. I
wake up and Jackie is covered in my coat, his coat,
socks—anything to warm him. One day Mrs. Parson
brings a quilt. Squares of yellow, squares of blue. *Bundle
me up Jackie.* Now I don't need him for warm. I need him
for Mummy.

Mummy is up there on the dresser. In a Sunday blouse, in a tin frame. Beside Mummy—the X's. Jackie's made a calendar. One X for each gone day. It goes up to the twelfth of December—that's how long Mummy has to come get us before they give us away. I can't count. Jackie says that's lucky. Lucky for me.

The Barnardo man comes. He comes in fall. He's not the same as the one who picked us up in the motor car and sent us to Kingskettle. And he is the same. He's got a little blue suit too. He's got Jesus in a frame. He's got a book with both our names spelt grown up. But he don't want both our names.

He only wants Jackie's.

The Barnardo man tells Jackie that Jackie will go to Canada in four days. The man don't want to see the X's in our room. He shows Jackie something in his book. He don't see how Jackie goes still. How Jackie won't look at me now, how Jackie turns away.

The day come for Jackie to go. Jackie's got a plan. He makes me a promise. There's another boat come springtime. If Mummy still hasn't come he'll send me passage to Canada. He'll save every single penny, every single day.

I walk with Jackie to the train station. Chug-ah chug-ah ... Jackie climbs up the train. *Run back home now Katie. Run home all the way.*

And I do. I run. But I don't run back home. I run for that train. I run for Jackie.

14

The sound of wind, we see it moving through the hay.

KATIE runs hard, toward the house, toward ALISTAIR, who looks out through his bedroom window, toward KATIE.

Black out.

ACT ONE

Scene One

Summer, the present, afternoon in the kitchen of Alistair's farmhouse. EWAN pores over the instructions and starts to assemble a pot rack as FLORA grows impatient looking for something in her cupboards.

FLORA

You know your sister. She'll do it all in one go. Maybe she'll stop in that place outside Brockville because it's easy to get off the highway there—but only if she needs the little girls' room. Or a sandwich. But I'll bet you a million dollars she'll do the whole thing in one go. She's smart, Lorna.

EWAN

I didn't know driving from Toronto to Cornwall was a sign of intelligence.

FLORA

Now I can exit but I don't like getting back on board. Re-entry is not my strong point. Lorna'd drive to the moon if she could. She's smart.

EWAN

A genius. The whole 401—teeming with geniuses.

EWAN holds the pot rack up, more or less together.

EWAN

Well Auntie Flora. There you go. There's your pot rack.

FLORA

(*pause*) So that's it then.

EWAN

It is.

FLORA

Well I wouldn't exactly call it pretty. What do you suppose it's for then?

EWAN

You hang your pots from it.

FLORA

I don't want my pots and pans displayed to the nation! Put it out back.

EWAN

If someone gives you something stupid for your birthday you tell them "thank you but no." You've had this dumb thing in a box for two years.

FLORA

I enjoy things that are new. And I like keeping new things in their box.

EWAN

It's Lorna for Christ sakes. You could've told her you didn't need a pot thing.

FLORA
That doesn't mean I can be rude. It was kind of Lorna
to think of me.

EWAN
A couple of years ago you gave me a shirt that was too
small. So I took it back. Tell me Auntie Flora—was that
being rude?

FLORA
You could've lost a bit of weight. Then you could've
worn the shirt and felt better about yourself ... You
better not have taken my gravy boat. I've been looking
for it high and low.

EWAN
What would I want with a gravy boat?

FLORA
You tell me. And if it wasn't you who took it then it was
someone else.

EWAN
A robber's going to come all the way out here and then
down half a mile of gravel to steal your gravy boat.

FLORA
People are crazy. It was for the cheese sauce, for my
impossible broccoli pie.

EWAN
Lorna won't want dairy either. Bet you a million dollars.
She's probably still micro-idiotic.

FLORA
Don't tell your father about her not eating dairy. He'll
hit the roof.

EWAN
Why?

FLORA
Well this is a dairy farm now, isn't it?

EWAN
In case you hadn't noticed there hasn't been a cow
around here for twenty years.

FLORA
And if you bring up quotas or the milk board or any of
that I'll hit the roof.

(*looking at the pot rack*) Well I could hang the pressure
cooker from it. You better not have burned macaroni in
that one.

EWAN
And that's it then? Just one pot?

FLORA
And my kettle. Lorna sent it when she couldn't come
last Christmas.

EWAN
It's electric. You're not supposed to hang electrical
appliances off 'a here.

FLORA
It's not my fault that every pot in this house's got a
burnt up bottom! You and your late-night cooking. You
and Wesley cooked a steak in corn syrup once.

EWAN
Auntie Flora—that was thirty years ago. Mum forgave
me the next day.

FLORA
Poor Teenie—

EWAN
There was nothing poor about Mum. She charged me
nine dollars for that frying pan.

ALISTAIR
(*off*) FLORA!

FLORA
There we go again. The master's voice. Little Johnny
Mac came by with the milk this morning and he thought
it was Wesley ...

> *ALISTAIR has entered. EWAN and FLORA are unsure*
> *whether or not ALISTAIR has overheard.*

ALISTAIR
The box is full of swimmers.

FLORA
Rockford is on CRT at noon. Same as he was yesterday
and a thousand yesterdays before that.

ALISTAIR
Well someone let Rockford out 'ta the box.

FLORA
If he's not on now he'll be on A&E at one. And on
prime at one o'clock as well. If you still haven't found
Rockford you'll get him on thirty-nine at two.

EWAN
All *Rockford Files*, all day long.

ALISTAIR
I like him in this time zone.

FLORA
CRT. Channel forty-three. Same time, same station,
every day of the week.

ALISTAIR
You get him. Use your flipper.

FLORA
I got you a big button flipper on purpose so you could
use it yourself.

ALISTAIR
If that's what you call a big button flipper I'd hate to see
a little one.

FLORA
Biggest button flipper in all of Sears.

EWAN
Auntie Flora—you need anything in Cornwall?

FLORA
A gravy boat.

ALISTAIR
She needs Rockford back where he belongs.

EWAN
I'll take that as a no.

FLORA
Don't you forget your father's suit at the drycleaners.
And your pants.

ALISTAIR
Last time Lorna wore pants to church.

FLORA

It was a pant suit dear. You make it sound like she come straight from the barn.

ALISTAIR

She's no interest in what happens in the barn, I'll tell you that.

EWAN exits.

FLORA

We'll see my gravy boat on Sunday night. We'll see it on the *Antiques Roadshow.* They'd love to get hold of my mother's dishes.

ALISTAIR

Sell all our junk to the box. Fine with me.

FLORA

You go back to your chair Alistair. I'll get your lunch in a minute. I want to finish getting out my dishes for Lorna.

ALISTAIR

Couldn't be bothered to visit in three years and she gets the good dishes—

FLORA

Don't you dare talk mean. She's your only daughter.

ALISTAIR

She's not your daughter. I don't know why you're making such a fuss.

FLORA

She's my only niece. I can't wait for Lorna to come. Back in your chair then.

ALISTAIR
Well she won't be here 'til after supper. Any fool knows
that.

FLORA
The dishes aren't for Lorna's supper tonight. I want the
good dishes for noon dinner tomorrow.

ALISTAIR
You set the table a day before we eat now?

FLORA
We'll all be in church for the kirkin' before dinner,
won't we? The church'll be full right up.

ALISTAIR
I'll stay out in the car then. Fine with me.

FLORA
No sir. We do this for Tina. Didn't she love the kirkin'?
And it's all we got now to bring Lorna home.

ALISTAIR
Don't hold your breath waiting for Lorna.

FLORA .
She'll be here before we know it.

ALISTAIR
Don't hold your breath.

Scene Two

*Late evening, LORNA enters dragging her bags behind her,
she looks at the house, at a light that brightens in Alistair's
bedroom window then goes out abruptly. LORNA hesitates
on the porch.*

Lights fade as time passes.

*

*The next morning, lights come up full and bright,
LORNA is sleeping on the porch. ALISTAIR enters, he is
wearing his good shirt, tie and suspenders. He stares at
LORNA impatiently, he bangs something abruptly and
LORNA opens her eyes.*

LORNA
Dad—

ALISTAIR
We got eleven places to sleep in this house.

LORNA
Good morning to you too ... I just felt like sleeping on
the porch.

ALISTAIR
I count the chesterfields.

LORNA
It wasn't personal.

ALISTAIR
I figure them in.

LORNA
It was too hot to sleep in my room.

ALISTAIR
Hotter in Toronto.

LORNA
Last time there was some kind of motor on the floor in
fifty million pieces.

FLORA enters.

FLORA
I told him not to wake you up! Did he wake you up?

LORNA
Auntie Flora.

LORNA and FLORA embrace, FLORA is overcome.

ALISTAIR
She'd sleep 'til noon if you give her the chance—

FLORA
God love us you're like you're mother. Isn't she just like
Teenie?

FLORA is overcome again.

LORNA
How are you?

FLORA
What time did you get in last night? I was dead to the
world—

ALISTAIR
Ten fifty-three.

FLORA
You're still in that little house by the subway? You and
Stevie?

LORNA
I'm still in the house. Stevie's living with his dad.

ALISTAIR
Eh?

LORNA
(*beat*) For the summer.

FLORA ushers LORNA into the kitchen, ALISTAIR follows.
EWAN is finishing a cup of coffee.

EWAN
You got old, Lorna. Old and wrinkly.

LORNA thumps her brother on the head.

LORNA
Shut up.

EWAN and LORNA embrace.

ALISTAIR
What would you get now for that little house?

LORNA
I don't know. Two or three hundred thousand dollars.

FLORA
Good gracious.

EWAN
A rich divorcee. The guys must be lining up around the block.

FLORA
I'm sure Lorna doesn't appreciate you bringing up her marriage difficulties.

ALISTAIR
Difficulties she says?

FLORA

Do you Lorna?

ALISTAIR

God damn disaster that.

FLORA

(*pause*) Go get your good pants on Ewan. I want to see if they need pressing

EWAN

They just came from the drycleaners—

FLORA

You heard me.

> *EWAN and FLORA exit. An awkward pause, ALISTAIR longs to visit with his daughter but he barely knows how.*

LORNA

So Auntie Flora's still looking after you?

ALISTAIR

I don't need anyone looking after me—

LORNA

It's what she does Daddy. With Grandma and Grandpa. And then when Mum got sick—

ALISTAIR

She come to visit in 1990. We still got no idea when she's going to leave ...

You hear what happened across the road there?

LORNA

At MacIlwane's?

ALISTAIR
Gone. Some from Sherbrooke bought it. They live in the barn. Hired a crew come from Montreal. Made them a bedroom in the hayloft. MacIlwane's real house they turned into a cottage. They call it "the cottage." Ewan made them a sign out of cherry wood. Charged them seventy-four dollars. Know what it says?

LORNA
The cottage.

ALISTAIR
You ever meet anyone from that Milk Board down there in Toronto?

LORNA
No.

ALISTAIR
Maybe they're all too ashamed to say what they do. All of them on the Milk Board.

LORNA
They probably wear a disguise of some sort.

> *FLORA enters carrying little swatches of tartan. She tries to pin a tartan onto ALISTAIR's shirt. FLORA admires the tartan.*

FLORA
This tartan's Hunting MacEachern.

ALISTAIR
Go stick your pins in someone else.

FLORA
'Member last year you wore the MacEachern dress tartan.

It's a bit cheeky, the dress. Not like the Ancient
MacEachern.

LORNA

What does it look like, Dad?

FLORA

Alistair? It'd be like the MacEachern dress but faded. Eh
Alistair?

ALISTAIR

I wouldn't know. Where's my bucket?

FLORA

Don't tell me you're going to the barn in your nice
clothes.

ALISTAIR

All right, I won't tell you.

LORNA

You want some company, Dad?

ALISTAIR

I want you to get ready for church.

LORNA

We've still got three hours—

ALISTAIR

Don't you dare be late!

LORNA

You got little kittens in the barn?

ALISTAIR

Ewan's got himself a horse. She's an awful contraption.

FLORA

Penny. She's twenty-seven.

LORNA
What's Ewan doing with a twenty-seven-year-old horse?

ALISTAIR
Not one god damn thing. I might give her to one of Wesley's boys next door there. They love their horses. Might shoot her.

LORNA
How is Wes?

ALISTAIR
Gone to Prince Edward Island.

FLORA
No sir. They come home last night. They're coming here to dinner after church.

ALISTAIR
Eh?

FLORA
Not the whole brood. Just Wesley and his mother.

LORNA
What were they doing back east?

FLORA
A big meeting. A big party for the home children.

LORNA
Did you know about it Dad?

ALISTAIR starts putting the table scraps into a bucket.

FLORA
He's no interest dear.

ALISTAIR
Big lot of complaining. That's what goes on at those
meetings.

LORNA
How would you know if you don't go to anything?

ALISTAIR
Rather shovel shit in the barn than listen to that lot.

FLORA
Now, now … We'll let Dorrie and Wesley tell us all about
it.

ALISTAIR
And we don't need Dorrie MacGillvray come to our
house to eat our food and tell us a thing.

FLORA
We haven't had company since Christmas. Tell your dad
to behave himself Lorna.

LORNA
You tell him.

FLORA hands a piece of MacEachern tartan to LORNA.

FLORA
There you go Miss MacEachern.

LORNA
I've always liked the MacEachern tartan.

FLORA then gives LORNA a piece of MacKenzie tartan.

FLORA
This one is Ancient MacKenzie. You wear that for your
mother.

LORNA
I'm proud to be a MacKenzie too.

FLORA
You wear it over your heart at the service today. But make sure you hide it. You don't let anyone see your tartan until the Reverend gives you the word to bring it out for the blessing.

LORNA
I know the drill.

FLORA
Your poor mum ... Didn't Tina love the kirkin'?

ALISTAIR
Aye that she did.

FLORA recites the family prayer.

FLORA
"Bless the MacKenzies and the MacKenzie children, their sons and sons' children, and their daughters, for a thousand years to come."

LORNA
What about the daughters' children? Why don't they make it into the MacKenzie prayer?

FLORA
I'm sure the daughter's children are blessed too.

LORNA
My kid could use a prayer same as the next guy—

FLORA
They're just not in the official version.

ALISTAIR
He not want to come here then, your boy?

LORNA
His name's Stephen.

ALISTAIR
I know his name.

LORNA
He doesn't want to do anything. He's sixteen. He is not a civilized person ... Do the MacEacherns have a prayer?

ALISTAIR
No sir.

LORNA
Figures.

FLORA
That can't be true. They'd have a prayer, the MacEacherns, same as anyone else.

LORNA gives ALISTAIR a little hug, he freezes.

LORNA
Good to see you Daddy.

LORNA exits.

FLORA
I learned the MacKenzie prayer when I was ten years old. All the clans have their prayers. Even the MacEacherns.

ALISTAIR
They all pray for the MacKenzies to stop talking.

Scene Three

A few hours later, DORRIE and ALISTAIR are having tea after their noon dinner. ALISTAIR and DORRIE are uncomfortable with the silence and with each other. DORRIE doesn't look at ALISTAIR.

DORRIE
I'll tell you why we didn't see Sadie MacGregor at the kirking. She went into the Manor on Wednesday. They'd been waiting for a bed to open up for Sadie since March. They'd been told they might have to wait 'til next winter.

ALISTAIR
Flu season.

DORRIE
She got Little Donny Dan's bed. So Little Donny's gone now too. Gone to a better place.

ALISTAIR
Gone somewheres ...

FLORA enters with dessert, EWAN follows. A moment later LORNA enters with cell phone in hand, she is talking to Stephen.

LORNA
I don't know how much. Just tell your dad to call me ... Stephen! ... Shit!

LORNA puts away her phone.

FLORA
How's Stevie?

LORNA

You don't want to know.

DORRIE

Sadie's got the room right beside Mabel. Poor Mabel's
still paralyzed on that one side, head to toe ... Got a
ribbon tied round her leg. The right leg. That's the one
that don't work cause of the stroke.

FLORA

Why they tie up Mabel's leg?

DORRIE

It's to remind Mabel that the leg belongs to her. I guess
every time Mabel turned over on her side she kept
thinking she had someone else's leg, lying there on top
of her. She don't know it's attached to her because she
don't feel it. It'd scare me half to death—an unknown
leg.

ALISTAIR sticks his fingers into dessert.

FLORA

Get your fingers out of there mister!

ALISTAIR

I didn't hardly eat any dinner. It was all cold.

FLORA

It was supposed to be. It was a summer dinner. I
would've done a hot dinner but I'm without a gravy
boat ... We'll give you a plate, Dorrie, to take home for
Wesley.

LORNA

Why wasn't Wes in church?

DORRIE
He's got a heifer giving him some trouble.

LORNA
You tell him I want to see him.

ALISTAIR
It's too late for calving—

DORRIE
Well whatever it is Wesley's terrible busy. We shouldn't 'a gone out to the Maritimes. It put him behind. And I missed my appointment with Dr. Mootie.

FLORA
I couldn't survive without Dr. Mootie.

EWAN
Know what I think? You two got a little crush on your foot doctor.

FLORA
That's the silliest thing I ever heard of.

DORRIE
Not many doctors anymore who come right to the house.

FLORA
Dr. Mootie should 'a got the Order of Canada. Not that little French man over there in Hawkesbury.

ALISTAIR
She's talking sense for a change.

LORNA silences everyone with a look. Pause.

DORRIE
They'd a picture of the *S.S. Melita* at the reunion
Alistair.

ALISTAIR
Pass that muck there Ewan.

DORRIE
That's the boat we come on. Not at the same time of
course—

ALISTAIR
It's west 'a the teapot.

FLORA
Did you see some people you knew out there Dorrie?

DORRIE
Not a soul. It's more for the young people. Wesley
enjoyed it.

FLORA
He's clannish, Wesley.

DORRIE
He liked the speeches ... Not many of us left now. Right
Alistair—

ALISTAIR
A piper come down to the dock. Played "Oh Canada"
for the Chinese.

LORNA
What Chinese?

ALISTAIR
The ones in the dirty boat. Out there in B.C. Sneaking
their way in.

EWAN
He means the migrants.

ALISTAIR
From Fuji-wuji.

EWAN
From Fujian Province.

LORNA
Was there another boat?

EWAN
Yesterday afternoon. The third boat this summer.

ALISTAIR
Trying to sneak their way into the country! They come
in swimming. Come in swimming and gulping in their
red suits. They got Rockford all out of whack. They
ruined the schedule.

DORRIE
They'd a social worker there in the Maritimes, he come
from London. He worked for the Aid. He said if we ever
wanted to go back there to visit, to Britain, he'd send us
a ticket. Me and Wesley both. The government there,
they'll also help find any family.

LORNA
Could Dad do that? Go back to Edinburgh?

DORRIE
I'm sure he could. There was one poor chap there in
the Maritimes. He'd gone home to England last
summer and nobody knew him. Not a soul.

LORNA
Have you been back?

DORRIE
Well no.

LORNA
Why's that?

DORRIE
No one ever asked me to come.

ALISTAIR
They wouldn't know what to make of the bagpipes,
those Chinese.

FLORA
It'd be a welcome sound. The sound of the pipes.

ALISTAIR
The piper meant it for go home. Scat! Get back in your
awful boat.

LORNA
It would be interesting, Dad, to see if you have any
family left there in Scotland. I could look into it for you.
Even if you don't want to go there.

ALISTAIR
She wants a free trip on the airplane.

LORNA
No I don't.

FLORA
Your father's got a family, right here around the table.
Who wants more?

LORNA
I just thought you might want to find out more about
your family.

FLORA

We all know how your dad feels about that. None of
that's changed these last three years.

EWAN

Lorna bugging Dad about it hasn't changed either.

ALISTAIR

I know where my mother's buried. By that Presbyterian
church. On the High Road—

LORNA

What about your father? You don't know the first thing
about him.

ALISTAIR

That's ridiculous. That's a ridiculous thing to say.

LORNA

It's not your fault—

ALISTAIR

You go home.

LORNA

What?

EWAN

Dad—

ALISTAIR

Go home and look after your boy!

LORNA

His dad's looking after him.

ALISTAIR

That's your job.

LORNA
Zoltan is perfectly capable of—

ALISTAIR
Leaving your boy while you're off on holiday!

LORNA
Believe me—coming here is never my idea of a holiday.

FLORA
You settle down now Alistair. Lorna's just come.

ALISTAIR
First she runs out on her husband—

LORNA
I knew this would happen.

ALISTAIR
Then she leaves the boy, all on his own! You think that's looking after him eh? Talking on the phone?

    LORNA is on her feet.

ALISTAIR
    That's it. There she goes.

EWAN
    Knock it off, Dad.

ALISTAIR
    Out the door.

EWAN
    Lorna, don't.

    LORNA pushes past her father, he points a finger at her, she stops in her tracks.

FLORA
    Alistair, she just come—

ALISTAIR
Don't you tell me I don't know nothing about my own father!

LORNA
Then tell me about him. Tell me one thing.

Pause. LORNA exits.

FLORA
Why don't you go lie down Alistair.

ALISTAIR
I come up ...

FLORA
Nice and cool there in the summer kitchen.

ALISTAIR
I come up ... I come up to his middle.

Scene Four

Twilight, ALISTAIR is sitting on the side of his bed, looking out at the field. Lights fade then come up on LORNA, in the near dark, cutting through the edge of the field. LORNA walks toward the house. WESLEY is sitting on the porch. He calls out to her.

WESLEY
What do you think you're doing? Out there tramping on the hay?

LORNA stops, stares at WESLEY. She is pleased to see him.

LORNA
I went for a walk.

WESLEY
Nine-hour walk. This is the country for god's sake. You aren't supposed to walk anywhere.

LORNA
Hey Wes.

WESLEY
Hello darlin'.

LORNA has arrived at the porch. WESLEY and LORNA embrace warmly. EWAN enters.

WESLEY
Your brother here was ready to call in the army.

EWAN
No I wasn't.

LORNA
You think Dad'll let me back in the house?

EWAN
Why can't you just ignore him? It works for me—

LORNA
Nothing works here. Not since Mum died.

EWAN lights a joint, offers some to LORNA and WESLEY, they both decline.

LORNA
No thank you.

LORNA shoots EWAN a disapproving look.

EWAN
There's the LOOK. The God-Almighty-Holier-Than-Thou Look. I HATE that look.

LORNA
Well I hate it here.

EWAN
Why'd you come then?

LORNA
You told me to!

WESLEY
I'll have a beer, Ewan. Go get me a beer.

EWAN
Get your own beer.

WESLEY exits.

LORNA
You smoke every night?

EWAN
If at all possible. Yes I do.

LORNA

And at work?

EWAN

Not while operating heavy equipment, just like the label says.

LORNA

I'm going home in the morning.

EWAN

Suit yourself.

LORNA

I can't put up with Dad's bullshit anymore. I'm not like you.

EWAN

Why don't you haul Dad back down to Toronto and live with him for a few decades? Maybe then we can have a discussion about just what it is I have to put up with.

LORNA

I appreciate what you do for him.

EWAN

You don't know shit about what I do for him.

LORNA

And I appreciate what you do for Auntie Flora. I do.

EWAN

(*pause*) Then stay a couple of days.

LORNA

I don't know—

EWAN

This will probably be your last visit with him.

LORNA
    Why?

EWAN
    What do you mean why? He's old Lorna. Old and
    stupid.

        *WESLEY enters, hands LORNA a beer and opens one for
        himself.*

WESLEY
    You talking about me?

        WESLEY sits beside LORNA.

WESLEY
    You always bring the excitement with you Lorna
    Kathleen … You tell her about Josette?

        EWAN shakes his head.

LORNA
    Tell me about Josette.

WESLEY
    Wild little French girl. Come from Lancaster. Very nice
    girl truth be told.

LORNA
    You deserve somebody nice.

WESLEY
    That's true but I can't stay away from the mean ones. It's
    Ewan's got Josette.

LORNA
    Josette's your girlfriend?

EWAN
    Sort of. I guess so.

LORNA
That's amazing.

EWAN
You know I have to say—being this shocked that I might
have a girlfriend? It isn't flattering.

LORNA
Why didn't you tell me?

EWAN
I don't like rubbing stuff in people's faces.

LORNA
What? That you have one girlfriend every twelve years?

EWAN
She's got a bunch of kids. I'm not going to move in or
anything.

LORNA
How old is she?

EWAN
Forty-two.

    LORNA shoves WESLEY.

LORNA
Forty-two is not a little girl.

WESLEY
I still call you a little girl.

LORNA
Well don't.

WESLEY
I hear you left what's-his-name.

LORNA
He left me.

WESLEY
He was a prick Lorna, an arrogant prick. Zipper.

LORNA
Zoltan.

WESLEY
An arrogant prick with a stupid name.

LORNA
He's got a girlfriend.

WESLEY
She young?

LORNA
No. And she's way nicer than me.

WESLEY
Let me cook you supper tomorrow. I'll give you some pointers on being divorced.

LORNA
I'm going home—

WESLEY
Don't do that Lorna. You'll break his heart.

LORNA
Whose heart?

WESLEY touches the piece of tartan over LORNA's heart.

LORNA
It's for my mother.

WESLEY
Wearing your tartan ten hours after the service—

LORNA

Why weren't you in church? They had the lone piper and the procession of tartans.

WESLEY

I hate that stuff—

LORNA

Then the minister blessed all the clans, one by one.

WESLEY

It's bullshit—the kirkin' o' the tartan. They don't go off kirkin' stuff in Scotland.

LORNA

1746. The tartans were banned. It's a fact.

WESLEY

An American minister come up with the idea during the war. He invented this stupid ceremony to get men with roots in the old country riled up to go overseas and fight ... People love the kirking so much that they want it to be true.

LORNA

I want it to be true.

WESLEY

No Highlander ever snuck their tartan into church to receive a blessing. But no one seems to care that it never really happened. Everyone pretends we have this history. Jesus—Mum's from England and she trots right up there with the rest of them. But look at her. Look at your dad. And you should 'a seen that old bunch out there in the Maritimes ... There's our history. Eighty thousand children come from Britain to Canada and were placed in slavery—

LORNA
They were orphans—

WESLEY
Not all of them. Not by a long shot ... Look at Casanova
there.

*EWAN has fallen asleep. LORNA places her jacket around
EWAN.*

LORNA
Getting stoned every night. He'll probably burn this
whole place down ...

WESLEY
They gave us a big package of Barnardo junk in the
Maritimes to take home—pictures from the homes,
passenger lists. Ever since we got it Mum's been packing
it around like a god damn doll. You should take a look
at it.

LORNA
Why didn't we ever talk about this stuff?

WESLEY
No one talked about it. Someone even asks Mum where
she's from and she gets this look. Her face clouds over
in two seconds flat. And she's gone, shut down, even if
she's sitting right there in front of you. I've been seeing
that look ever since I can remember. This weekend was
the first time she got asked that question and it was
okay. She was with her tribe.

LORNA
Dad doesn't want anything to do with any of them. He
never has. Stevie did a project on the home children in

grade five and Dad wouldn't help. He wouldn't give his own grandson the time of day.

WESLEY
You know I've seen your dad lately down in our east field. Down there by the highway.

LORNA
Doing what?

WESLEY
I don't know. Just admiring the view …

LORNA
He's weird. And getting weirder, especially since Mum died.

WESLEY
How long since your mum died?

LORNA
Ten years.

WESLEY
Jesus. It feels like less than ten years since we were in high school, rolling around in the hayloft …

LORNA
You're shameless. Did you know that?

WESLEY puts his arm around LORNA.

WESLEY
I told Mum I'm writing to the Prime Minister on her behalf. We're going to demand compensation. The idea of it almost gave her a heart attack.

LORNA
Poor Dorrie.

WESLEY
She's been trained her whole life not to make a fuss.
The whole bunch of them have. And when she's gone
and your dad's gone. And that handful of old men and
women I met out there in Prince Edward Island, when
they're all gone … Know what's going to be left?
Nothing. Zero. Not a ripple.

Scene Five

A few hours later, lights up on EWAN in the kitchen in the half dark. He has just raided the fridge. Suddenly ALISTAIR is right there, in his pyjamas and bare feet, frantic and disoriented.

ALISTAIR
You see her?

EWAN
Who?

ALISTAIR
That girl.

EWAN
Haven't seen a girl.

ALISTAIR
You tell her ... You tell her to walk down the side.

EWAN
Are you okay Dad? I heard you crashing around there upstairs—

ALISTAIR
Stay off the middle of the tracks!

EWAN
Will do. I was just getting something to eat. What are you doing up so late?

ALISTAIR looks around, he is trying to get his bearings.

ALISTAIR
Going milking.

EWAN
It's three in the morning.

ALISTAIR
Time to get up.

EWAN
You don't have any cows.

ALISTAIR
What'd I do to them?

EWAN
You sold them to that Dutch man. Over there at
Vankleek Hill. You want to go up to your bed then? You
need a hand on the stairs? It's not safe for you walking
around here in the middle of the night.

ALISTAIR
You smell a' fire.

EWAN
I had a cigarette. You know, once in a while. Don't tell
Auntie Flora.

ALISTAIR
I can't go with you.

EWAN
Sure you can. We just got to go up the stairs.

ALISTAIR
Eh?

EWAN
I've got to get you back to bed.

ALISTAIR
If you see that Katie on the middle of the tracks?

EWAN
Uh—huh—

ALISTAIR
You give her a swat.

EWAN
No thanks.

ALISTAIR
Do you hear?

EWAN
I can hear you all right. I just don't know what you're
talking about.

ALISTAIR hits EWAN on the side of the head.

EWAN
Jesus, what are you doing?

*ALISTAIR looks around the room, he is back in the present
and very worried.*

EWAN
Dad? Do you hear me?

ALISTAIR
What'd I do?

EWAN
You hit me. That's what you did.

ALISTAIR
I wouldn't do that to you.

EWAN
Well you did. You're all mixed up Dad. You're all sweaty.
I'm going to help you back up the stairs. You need to go
back to sleep. Don't hit me.

ALISTAIR
I can't see nothing.

EWAN
I know. It's the middle of the night.

ALISTAIR
Lorna's here.

EWAN
That's right.

ALISTAIR
She's a good girl Lorna.

ALISTAIR turns to join EWAN, he walks face first into FLORA's pressure cooker, hanging off the pot rack. He goes down, EWAN runs to him, prods him, urging him up. ALISTAIR appears to be dead weight.

EWAN
Dad? You okay? Can you hear me? Dad!

Scene Six

*Two days later, lights up in the kitchen, FLORA speaks off
to EWAN.*

FLORA

A big stroke was on its way, whether or not I hung up
that darn pressure cooker.

It's 'cause it's new—I just had to show it off. It's the
only pot I got that you never burnt on me. Now I'm not
saying it's your fault either. These things just happen ...
Oh I can't stand to see poor Alistair lying there all still
and quiet! They got the wrong man. That's what I keep
thinking. They got the wrong man stuck there in that
poor old body.

EWAN enters.

EWAN

The doctor said the stroke probably started way before
Dad came downstairs.

FLORA

I've got a bad feeling about all this Ewan.

EWAN

He's not ready to peg out yet.

FLORA

That left side still won't work. Can't hardly open his eye
on that side. Same as Mabel and Mabel's been like that
eight months. The poor soul. And he's so mixed up. He
can't figure out if I'm Tina. Then I'm Lorna. Poor
Lorna come all this way to see her dad, now this ...

EWAN

At least she's sticking around.

FLORA

Alistair still doesn't have his teeth in. He's lost his way.
He has lost his way.

EWAN

Everyone looks lost without their teeth in.

FLORA

Did you talk yet to that oriental fellow in the bed next
door? Now he had a stroke a month ago and he's
getting his feeling back.

EWAN

There you go then.

FLORA

Mr. Tang. Like the orange juice. He don't eat the
hospital food. His children bring his meals in those little
Tupperware dishes. Poor Alistair gets his dinner in a
tube hooked up to his hand.

EWAN

That'll change soon.

 LORNA enters.

FLORA

How is he?

LORNA

I had the meeting with his neurologist. Which means I
waited in the hall three hours for some guy to talk to me
for two seconds.

EWAN

What'd he say?

LORNA
We just have to keep waiting. See how much comes
back. He's sitting up now.

FLORA
That's a good sign. Did he know you?

LORNA
Sort of. Except he thinks I'm Mum sometimes. And
Katie. Who's Katie?

FLORA
Katie …

EWAN
He talked to me about Katie too.

LORNA
There's a switch, Auntie Flora. Someone you don't
know.

EWAN
Katie MacMillan. Archie Dawe's wife. Do you figure?

FLORA
Why would he be talking about Mrs. Archie Dawe?

EWAN
That's for Dad to know and us to figure out.

FLORA
Don't you go spreading rumours about poor Alistair
and Mrs. Archie Dawe! She's ninety-four. Are you
hungry Lorna?

LORNA
I'm fine.

EWAN

I'll have a piece of that banana bread Dorrie sent over.

FLORA

You eat too many sweets! Last night you ate up that old
square that was supposed to go out to the chickens ...
Everyone sending in baking like he's already gone.
When poor Tina died we ate frozen cake for a year and
a half.

LORNA

I'm glad Mum's dead.

FLORA

Don't say that Lorna.

LORNA

I'm glad she doesn't have to see him like this.

FLORA

Cancer like your mum had—that's a terrible thing. But
strokes—they're mean. Mean as can be.

LORNA

Where are the papers that were on the table this
morning? You know all those papers Dorrie lent me
from her reunion?

FLORA

Out by the phonebooks. We had no room to eat. Did we
Ewan?

Lorna retrieves the papers.

LORNA

You should look at this stuff sometime.

EWAN

Why?

LORNA

Why? Because it's interesting. Don't worry. You don't
have to read anything. Just look at the pictures. The
pictures are fantastic.

*Lights up on ALISTAIR, lying on a hospital bed. As the
lights begin a slow fade on the kitchen, they warm on
ALISTAIR. KATIE enters, she peers over the side of
ALISTAIR's bed.*

KATIE

Jackie ... Jackie? You awake?

FLORA examines the photographs.

FLORA

I'll tell you one thing. You could always tell a homeboy a
mile away. In the back row there at church. Standing in
their own little group at a social. Going through the
world in their own little boat. In the old days you'd see
their tin trunks and their names pinned to their jackets.
You'd see them at the train stations. And I thought they
were lucky. Because they got to cross the Atlantic Ocean
in a boat.

*ALISTAIR reaches out a hand toward KATIE, tries to prop
himself up and fails.*

KATIE

You're all cold there Jackie.

ALISTAIR

Co Co Co ...

FLORA

Dorrie said they slept four to a cot on the boat coming
over. The poor little souls.

KATIE climbs over the bed rails, wraps herself tight around ALISTAIR.

KATIE
I'll bundle you up Jackie.

FLORA
Imagine that ... All those children, down in the hold.

Scene Seven

The next morning, the hospital, KATIE is sitting on the end of ALISTAIR's bed. ALISTAIR is asleep. KATIE swings her feet back and forth waking up ALISTAIR. He is startled to see her. Lights shift as he goes back in time, back to the train, to the last time he has seen her.

ALISTAIR
You get off!

KATIE
I won't.

ALISTAIR
Katie! You gct offa' this train or I'll call the conductor! The conductor'll put you in jail.

KATIE
No sir.

ALISTAIR kicks KATIE off the end of the bed. She lands hard on the floor. KATIE starts to wail.

ALISTAIR
Shut up! Shut up! You're no' a baby—

KATIE
Jackie's a baby!

ALISTAIR
You're out at the next stop. You follow the train tracks right back to Kingskettle. You walk on the side, not down the middle. Hear?

KATIE
I'll hide under the seat. The conductor'll no' see me.

ALISTAIR

That your plan then?

KATIE

Aye. All the way to Canada.

ALISTAIR

This train's no' going to Canada you stupid girl. No
train goes right to Canada. It goes to London. And then
a big boat and a big crossing.

KATIE

That's no' true. Mrs. Parsons, Mrs. Parsons said—

ALISTAIR

Canada's across the sea.

KATIE

Jackie! There's a bridge. A bridge from Scotland to
Canada for the boys and the girls!

ALISTAIR

There is no' a bridge.

KATIE

A bridge a' gold! Mrs. Parsons said.

ALISTAIR

Mrs. Parsons is fat and stupid. You no listen to Mrs.
Parsons. You listen to me.

KATIE

Scads a' children. Thousands ... They come across the
sea, they come on the bridge. When Mummy comes to
Kingskettle, when she comes to fetch us ... She won't be
allowed. No grown ups on the bridge. But we'll send her
passage. Save every single penny, every single day.

ALISTAIR

(*pause*) Mummy's not gonna come.

KATIE

On the boat Jackie. She'll come on the boat.

ALISTAIR

(*pause*) Mummy's gone to heaven from coughing.

KATIE

Who said that? Who told that to you?

ALISTAIR

The Barnardo man, he wrote it in his book. Plain as day.
Gone to heaven. So I'll go to Canada and get things set
up for you and me. But you let Mrs. Parsons look after
you good until I'm ready. There's a girl boat come this
spring.

ALISTAIR rips a button off his house coat.

ALISTAIR

You keep hold of this—just for you, from me. Keep hold
a' that until you see me. In spring there. Before you
know it.

The sound of a train whistle, the sound of brakes.

ALISTAIR

That's a cow having a piss.

KATIE

Is no' a cow.

ALISTAIR

Katie.

KATIE is starting to cry.

ALISTAIR
Go on now. Don't be sulky. Get offa' the train.

KATIE
NO!

ALISTAIR
You get offa' the train this minute! Or I'll throw you out the god damn window!

KATIE runs from ALISTAIR, exits. ALISTAIR lies back exhausted.

*

Lights shift back to the present. ALISTAIR is very upset, enter LORNA.

LORNA
Are you decent Dad?

ALISTAIR tries to prop himself up.

LORNA
How was your sleep?

ALISTAIR beckons LORNA to come close, he has a great deal of trouble trying to speak. He points toward where KATIE had been but LORNA, of course, doesn't see.

ALISTAIR
Go ...

LORNA
What's that?

ALISTAIR
Go ...

LORNA

I brought in the paper. You want me to read to you?
Auntie Flora thought you might like your lotion. Your
Vaseline.

*LORNA puts the container of moisturizer on the bed table.
She is nervous.*

*LORNA gently lifts the blanket off her father, his legs
bare, a ribbon tied around his leg.*

*LORNA rubs lotion into his feet, she is even more
nervous and ALISTAIR is still agitated.*

ALISTAIR

Go on—

LORNA

I'm not going to go.

*She continues to rub his legs. ALISTAIR starts to calm
down.*

LORNA

Look at you Daddy. All tied up with ribbon. You look
like a bride. When I was little I thought all the girls who
were waiting to get married went to the hall in
Dunvegan. Their faces were covered by a veil of cheese
cloth. And then the boys would come. They'd march up
and down in front of the girls. They'd lift the veil up
when they thought they'd found their one and only.
The girls who didn't get chosen went home to look after
the old people. Like Auntie Flora. Or they became
school teachers ... Like me.

Does that feel cold? Does that feel like anything?

LORNA touches the ribbon cautiously. ALISTAIR isn't aware of her touch. LORNA resumes on his good side.

ALISTAIR
Ka, Ka … Katie come.

LORNA
Katie.

ALISTAIR is growing upset again, he points to where KATIE had been.

ALISTAIR
There, there … Katie.

LORNA
You keep talking about Katie, Daddy.

ALISTAIR becomes more agitated, he points.

ALISTAIR
Go, go …

LORNA
Stop it. I'm not going to go. And there's no one here Dad. It's just you and me. Why is that so awful that it's just you and me?

ALISTAIR looks about, he realizes KATIE isn't here now but wants LORNA to know that she was here, moments ago.

ALISTAIR
Katie come to see me.

LORNA
You remember what Dorrie said about Mabel? She thought there was someone else in bed there with her after her stroke.

68

ALISTAIR
No.

LORNA
It's the weight of this side Dad, the one that's not
working. It feels like another person.

ALISTAIR
Katie.

LORNA
But it's you. It's just you that's here.

ALISTAIR is becoming very upset.

ALISTAIR
No—

LORNA
Do you feel her now? Is she here?

ALISTAIR fears now that KATIE has only been imagined.

LORNA
You probably just feel her when you're lying on this
side. That's what the ribbon's for. To remind you.

ALISTAIR
No, no—

ALISTAIR pulls hard at the ribbon to take it off.

LORNA
What are you doing? Just leave it Dad.

ALISTAIR
Katie. Katie come. My wee girl.

LORNA
I'm your wee girl Daddy, Lorna.

ALISTAIR
    My sister.

LORNA
    You don't have a sister.

ALISTAIR
    My sister, Katie.

LORNA
    You don't have a ...

ALISTAIR
    Go find her.

LORNA
    You have a sister?

ALISTAIR
    Don't let her get away.

LORNA
    What?

ALISTAIR
    Keep a' hold of her. Don't let her walk down the middle of the tracks. Katie.

End Act One.

ACT TWO

Scene One

KATIE sits cross-legged, at the edge of the field, mad at everybody, she looks toward ALISTAIR who sleeps in his hospital bed.

KATIE

I go to the post office. Every day after dinner. Mrs. Parsons walks slow. She gets all puffy. We stop at that bench. She eats bread and bacon from inside her purse.

When we get there, the Postmaster, he just shakes his head. I don't get nothing, Jackie, ever. No letters, not a one. Only thing we ever get is her books for knitting. Whoever heard of needing a book for knitting? She's an idiot Mrs. Parsons.

I tell her I know what happened to the letters. They've been stolen. *Who would steal Jackie's letters?* Indians I tell her. Why would an Indian want a letter written by your brother? An Indian, he wouldn't know how to read. It'll all be scratches to the Indians. She's an idiot Mrs. Parsons.

71

I get home. Nettie wants to know when it is we are leaving. We are both packed and ready for the boat. Nettie is a sock doll Mrs. Parsons made me for Christmas. I tell Nettie all the jokes you ever told me so I won't forget. I tell Nettie wait, hold your horses, one more day.

It comes. The letter comes right around Easter. Just like Jesus.

Mrs. Parsons says we have to wait 'til we get home to read it. But that Postmaster, he tells Mrs. Parsons to go sit in his chair. He'll read your letter to me.

You ... you said—I am not allowed to come to the farm where you're working. You said I am too little. You said one day you'll buy your very own farm for you and me.

The Post Master he pats my knee. He thinks I'm going to go off bawling. He doesn't know what I can do. What I can do better than anyone. You watch me Jackie. I can do it forever. I can wait.

Scene Two

One week later, late afternoon, lights up on WESLEY and
LORNA in the kitchen. They are at the table, papers
everywhere. WESLEY is reading while LORNA makes notes.
FLORA hovers.

WESLEY
"If the child came between 1919 and 1924 the
government used something called Form 30A."

LORNA
That might be too early. Dad can't remember what year
she came. He's still too mixed up.

FLORA
Don't you dare bother your father about this business.
His job now is to get well.

LORNA
He asked me to find her.

WESLEY
"If the child came between 1925 and 1935 then check
out the immigration database for those years." Write
that down; that's a job for Ewan.

FLORA
Poor Ewan's got enough on his plate. That Josette, she
keeps him hopping.

LORNA
We're just getting him to look up some things on his
laptop.

FLORA
His what?

LORNA
His computer, Auntie Flora.

FLORA
You won't find her in that little thing. You're not going to find her anywhere.

LORNA
And why is that?

FLORA
Because she's not real. If Alistair had a sister you'd think it might've come up in conversation once or twice in all these years.

WESLEY
There's all kinds of stories out there of siblings who got split up and never saw one another again—

FLORA
If my own sister knew of a little sister to Alistair she'd 'a told me.

WESLEY
Brothers who just assumed they'd be placed on a farm together and ended up three hundred miles apart.

FLORA
If you really want to do something for your dad, go visit and help him with his walking.

LORNA
He needs to learn how to use his walker.

FLORA
Alistair don't like his walker. He'd rather hold on to you or me.

LORNA
So you'll just let him hold your arm all day when he comes home.

FLORA
No bother to me.

LORNA
While you're baking bread or feeding your chickens—

FLORA
We'll all pitch in.

LORNA
I have to go home Auntie Flora.

WESLEY
When?

LORNA
School starts in two weeks. And I've got prep ... And Stevie.

WESLEY
When are you going?

FLORA
She's going on Friday.

WESLEY
I never got to make you supper.

LORNA
I'll come back for Thanksgiving.

FLORA
Your dad should be home by then.

WESLEY
So come over tonight.

FLORA
You go Lorna. Get away from all your papers.

WESLEY
We'll have a picnic.

LORNA
I want to finish checking the passenger lists.

WESLEY
I'll help you. You still have to eat.

FLORA
Bring Dorrie over to keep me company. Ewan'll be off with his French gal.

You two can have your picnic here.

WESLEY
You're on, Flora.

LORNA
"Check the child out in the '1' years. The years of the census. 1871, 1881, 1891"—

FLORA
So your Katie might be a hundred and thirty years old … Alistair went to a big house on Jarvis Street in Toronto when he first come.

LORNA
Thank you Auntie Flora. THAT was very useful.

FLORA

You're welcome. But I still don't believe in her for a
minute.

WESLEY

"Staff at Statistics Canada will answer inquiries
concerning individuals who have been deceased for
more than twenty years."

FLORA

You turn up a long-lost sister that's dead and I'll never
forgive you. Or maybe your Katie's a bad apple. Did you
ever think of that? Some of the children that come, they
weren't very pleasant.

LORNA

They were children.

FLORA

Our Charlie was polite as could be. But the second boy
we had ... Tina and me were scared to death of him. We
thought he was going to kill our dad.

WESLEY

And why would he want to do that?

FLORA

You tell me. And if you think for a second that my
mother and father were anything but decent to both
those boys and anyone else who come into our house—

WESLEY

I know that Flora. I didn't mean any disrespect to your
folks.

FLORA

All I know is that we had some pretty rough characters around here and that wasn't the fault of the Canadian farmer. Imagine taking home that boy with the hair we saw on St. Catherines Street. 'Member that boy?

WESLEY

I don't.

FLORA

Last November when you took your mother and me Christmas shopping to Montreal.

WESLEY

I have erased that day from my memory.

LORNA

You took Auntie Flora and your mum Christmas shopping?

WESLEY

I did.

LORNA

I will eat supper with you.

FLORA

You know that boy who asked us for money.

WESLEY

I remember.

FLORA

Bright blue hair sticking straight up on his head. I gave him twenty-five cents. He thought I was pretty cheap.

WESLEY

He didn't say a word to you.

FLORA
Exactly. Not a thank you, not even a smile. Maybe we should take all them teenagers sleeping on St. Catherines Street and ship them overseas.

LORNA
Auntie Flora—

FLORA
What? Now you're going to tell me to mind my own—

WESLEY starts to exit.

WESLEY
I'll come by around seven.

FLORA
It's a date.

WESLEY exits.

LORNA
You know if we find her, if we bring home Katie. That doesn't mean we shove you out the door.

FLORA
Well good golly. I know that.

LORNA
Then quit acting like you don't.

Enter EWAN.

LORNA
How's Josette?

EWAN
Good.

FLORA
Don't suppose we'll ever meet her.

EWAN
    Correct. I dropped in on Dad.

LORNA
    How is he?

EWAN
    He walked as far as the door today. Probably planning
    his escape ...

LORNA
    Something's wrong.

EWAN
    Don't panic.

LORNA
    I know you. Something's wrong.

FLORA
    Alistair's trying too much too soon. I could 'a told you
    that.

EWAN
    He wants us to stop.

LORNA
    Stop what?

EWAN
    This. Dad wants you to stop looking for Katie.

LORNA
    What?

FLORA
    She's just something the stroke brought on. I've been
    trying to tell you that.

LORNA

No she isn't.

EWAN

Auntie Flora's right.

LORNA

What did he say?

EWAN

That it was just talk. Junk. Talking crazy.

LORNA

You don't believe that ... do you?

FLORA

Little Donny Dan thought he was King a' Cornwall after
his stroke.

LORNA

He told me to look for her. It was real. She was real to
him. He told me to find Katie. And that's exactly what
I'm going to do.

EWAN

Why haven't you gotten anywhere? You've been at it for
nearly a week.

LORNA

I don't believe this.

FLORA

You said it yourself Lorna. There's no MacEacherns on
any of those lists.

EWAN

It doesn't matter if she's real or a piece of furniture. It's
Dad's business.

LORNA

> She's our aunt. Our family. And it's the first time Dad's
> asked me to do something for him, ever.

EWAN

> And now he's telling you to stop.

Scene Three

That evening, WESLEY sits on the porch. He speaks off to
LORNA.

WESLEY
After my dad's stroke he had this little notebook he
packed around with him. He wrote down all our names
to help him keep track of who we were. "I have four
sons. Robert, Dougie, Wesley and Willy. And fourteen
grandchildren. Wesley has two wives and is father to
Justin and Benny."

LORNA enters with a glass of wine for each of them.

WESLEY
Made me sound like a Mormon. Made me depressed
about my own life.

LORNA
You miss being married?

WESLEY
Sure I do. First time I was too young, second time I was
too stupid.

LORNA
I don't miss it.

WESLEY
You look like you do.

LORNA
What's that supposed to mean?

WESLEY
You always come out swinging, Lorna Kathleen.

LORNA
I'll bet I'm named after her, Katie ... I keep thinking of
this little girl. All by herself. Maybe she's been looking
for him, all these years. Maybe she's all messed up, like
Dad.

WESLEY
Your dad isn't a mess.

LORNA
How can you say that?

WESLEY
He had a good marriage, kids. He took over his in-laws'
farm. I remember your mum's folks.

LORNA
Grandpa wore an eye patch.

WESLEY
Got kicked by a cow.

LORNA
We were scared of him, of what might be under there ...

WESLEY
My dad's parents wouldn't give my mum the time of day.

*WESLEY stands behind LORNA. He wraps an arm around
her, he holds his hand against her forehead.*

LORNA
What are you doing?

WESLEY
Just relax, try to relax for a minute.

LORNA
Your hand is ... warm.

LORNA tries to relax.

WESLEY
That's better. Now shut your eyes. My hand, it's a poultice.

LORNA shuts her eyes.

WESLEY
Drawing all that hurt right out of you.

LORNA takes a deep breath, she starts to relax, to open a little.

LORNA
Maybe Katie doesn't remember Dad at all. Maybe he's just some old ache she doesn't understand.

WESLEY
We've all got those.

LORNA
Maybe Katie just—

WESLEY
Forget about Katie.

LORNA pulls away from WESLEY.

LORNA
I'm not going to do that.

WESLEY
I didn't mean forever.

LORNA
And don't think I'm some local girl you can use all your lines on.

WESLEY
I know that Lorna.

LORNA
And I know you. Tell me you haven't used that poultice
stuff before.

WESLEY
I'm fifty years old. I'm—

LORNA
A recycler.

WESLEY
Well yeah.

*LORNA turns to go in the house and DORRIE is right
there, her shoes in her hand.*

WESLEY
You're having some trouble there Mum?

DORRIE
I'm ruining your nice time with Lorna.

WESLEY
Can you get me a dishpan, Lorna? And fill it up with
warm water.

DORRIE
No, no.

LORNA
Where's Auntie Flora?

DORRIE
I sent her to bed.

LORNA exits.

DORRIE
It's a rotten business this.

WESLEY
Sit.

> *DORRIE sits. WESLEY begins to roll down her knee-high stocking.*

DORRIE
I wouldn't want anyone looking at these feet.

> *LORNA brings the pan of water. WESLEY put his mother's feet in it gently.*

WESLEY
You got a nasty corn there, Mum. When's your next date with Dr. Mootie?

DORRIE
Not 'til the end of next week.

WESLEY
I can file that off for you right this minute.

DORRIE
No sir.

WESLEY
I've been trimming hooves since I was nine years old.

DORRIE
Don't listen to him Lorna. The water'll fix me up just right.

WESLEY
You sit tight. I'm gonna bring the truck right up close.

> *WESLEY exits.*

LORNA
Can I make you a cup of tea?

DORRIE

I'm full of tea. I'm a big bother.

LORNA

Not for a minute.

DORRIE

Flora said Alistair called off the search.

LORNA

I'm still looking.

DORRIE

Because you believe there was a little girl.

LORNA

I do.

DORRIE

I do too Lorna.

LORNA

Thank you. That means a lot to me.

DORRIE

I'd 'a swum across the sea to see my own little sister ... I was working across the road there at MacIlwane's. First time in my life that I ever got a letter. It was from Barnardo's, telling me Winnie had died. Poor little thing.

LORNA

I'm sorry.

DORRIE

Your dad was there too, you know. At MacIlwane's.

LORNA

I didn't know you two worked together.

DORRIE

Just for one summer. They liked to ship us around ...
You know something? I don't give two hoots anymore
whether or not your dad gets mad at me.

LORNA

Why would Dad be mad at you?

DORRIE

An Irish boy come to help with the haying there at
MacIlwane's. He knew Alistair from a farm they were at
before, in Prescott. That boy wouldn't call Alistair
Alistair. He called him Jackie. Jackie Jack.

LORNA

Jackie?

DORRIE

Alistair told him to stop it. That wasn't his name no
more. A few days later I asked him about it. I was doing
up the dinner dishes and he was sitting there at the
table with his cup of tea. You know what he said? Who
hc was and where he come from wasn't none of my
business.

*WESLEY enters, as DORRIE speaks he rubs her feet gently
with a towel and puts on her stockings and shoes.*

DORRIE

Then he was up and out the door, quick as could be.
Until he married your mum I think that was the last
thing he ever said to me.

LORNA starts to go through the piles of paper on the table.

LORNA

Jackie.

DORRIE

You check your list for a Jack MacEachern or a John.

LORNA

I can't find any MacEacherns on the lists let alone a
Jackie MacEachern.

WESLEY

Then look for Jack or Jackson.

LORNA

I just did.

WELSEY

As a surname. Maybe his folks weren't married. Maybe
his legal name is different than how we know him.

LORNA scours her lists.

DORRIE

Isn't that a funny name? Jackie Jack.

LORNA throws down a stack of paper in frustration.

LORNA

No Jacksons, no Jacks.

DORRIE

Most of us didn't have any identification. And lots of the
boys, they couldn't write and they couldn't read.

LORNA

Jackman.

*LORNA stands up, circles her pile of papers for a moment
and then returns to it, searches the lists again and then
points with her finger, reads.*

LORNA
"Alistair Jackman and Kathleen Jackman, made property
of the Society of Waifs and Strays October 14, 1924 in
Edinburgh Scotland." Jackman ... Placed in a foster
home in Kingskettle Scotland in the care of a Mrs.
Beatrice Parsons."

LORNA jabs at a name on another list.

LORNA
Alistair Jackman. On the passenger list from the *S.S.
Melita.* The November crossing.

DORRIE
That's the boat he come on, same as me.

WESLEY
Bingo.

DORRIE
You think that's your dad?

LORNA seems frozen by the information.

WESLEY
Is Kathleen on that passenger list?

LORNA shakes her head.

LORNA
She might've come later.

DORRIE
Separate boats for the boys and the girls.

WESLEY
There's lots of lists to check ... Jackman. I'll be damned.

DORRIE
Jackman? You think that's your dad Lorna?

LORNA
I do.

DORRIE
But you're a MacEachern.

LORNA
At least I thought I was.

LORNA picks up her papers and heads for the door.

WESLEY
Why don't you sit down for a minute there Lorna.

LORNA
No.

WESLEY
Visiting hours ended a half hour ago.

LORNA stops.

LORNA
God damn him.

WESLEY
You don't know why he did what he did.

LORNA
Apparently I don't know anything about him.

WESLEY
You've got a name now. Kathleen Jackman.

LORNA
I lost my own name along the way.

WESLEY
I'll get Mum home then I'll come back and help you.
You've got her name. This is a good thing.

WESLEY embraces LORNA.

WESLEY
We can check passenger lists, records from Barnardo's, adoption registries. I'll stay. We'll work all night if we have to. We're going to find her. You're going to bring home Katie.

Scene Four

The next morning, lights up on ALISTAIR, at the hospital. His health improved but still very shaky, he is practicing walking with his walker, he yells off.

ALISTAIR

Hey! This thing here, the walker. It don't work right. You ever try driving a car with two wheels? You'd break your neck.

LORNA enters.

ALISTAIR

Give me a hand there Lorna. I hate this thing.

LORNA stares at ALISTAIR.

ALISTAIR

Never mind then.

ALISTAIR walks slowly to the bed using his walker, he sits.

LORNA

Alistair Jackman.

ALISTAIR

Eh?

LORNA

Also known as Jackie.

ALISTAIR

You're talking nonsense.

LORNA

That's your name. Also known as Jackie Jack. What's our name Dad? Our last name.

ALISTAIR

That's the craziest thing I ever been asked my whole life.

LORNA

Jackman.

ALISTAIR

(*pause*) Whoever told you that? They're a liar.

LORNA

Katie Jackman and Alistair Jackman.

ALISTAIR

Go home Lorna.

LORNA

She's posted her name. Katie. I found her. Now she's Jean. A Mrs. Jean Briggs. Adopted in Montreal when she was six years old.

ALISTAIR

Who's that?

LORNA

Katie! Your sister. She lives in British Columbia. And she's been looking, looking for you. She posted her name the very first year they started the Adoption Registry. That's years ago now. Years of waiting.

ALISTAIR

This is none of your business.

LORNA

My name is my business!

ALISTAIR

Don't you go near Katie.

LORNA

She's my aunt. We are going to write her a letter. Right now—you and me. And I'm going to send her a plane ticket.

ALISTAIR

You're not allowed.

LORNA

This didn't just happen to you! And it didn't just happen when you were a boy. It's happening right now to our family. To me!

ALISTAIR

You think I'm a bad daddy eh?

LORNA begins to write furiously.

LORNA

Dear Jean—

ALISTAIR

You don't know one god damn thing.

LORNA

My name is Lorna Katie MacEachern. I am the daughter of Alistair MacEachern.

ALISTAIR

You stop that.

ALISTAIR grabs at the paper, tries to rip it up.

LORNA

My father was born in Edinburgh Scotland in 1913. Alistair Jackman. Also known as Jackie Jack. Jackie.

Scene Five

Six weeks later, FLORA is setting the table for supper. EWAN is helping her, they are waiting for LORNA's arrival.

FLORA

Know what I found in the back bedroom? Right along side three of my good teacups? Full of bolts and screws?

EWAN

The gravy boat.

FLORA

The gravy boat.

EWAN

I was sorting—

FLORA

I don't want to hear about it.

EWAN

Good.

FLORA

Have you still got that old horse of yours in the front pasture?

EWAN

She likes the shade along the hedge.

FLORA

First thing company sees is that old sway back.

EWAN

Nobody's going to care about Penny.

FLORA looks out, she is very jumpy.

FLORA

They probably stopped at that place outside Brockville for coffee.

EWAN

They're not coming from Toronto. They're coming from Montreal. Lorna drove up there last night.

FLORA

Good golly. They're lost for sure then.

EWAN

They're not late Auntie Flora.

FLORA

They'll ask for directions at Saint Something-or-Other and no one will be able to speak to them in English ... Keep an ear out for your father. I don't want him to try and manage that shower all by himself.

EWAN

He didn't want a shower.

FLORA

We'll let him lie down right until they come or he'll be too worn out for dinner.

> *EWAN looks out.*

EWAN

They're here.

FLORA

Go get your dad right this minute!

EWAN

Would you settle down please.

EWAN exits. FLORA waits, she smoothes her hair, her dress.
LORNA finally enters, ushers in JEAN—a spry seventy-
seven-year-old, a hint of sophistication, but with
ALISTAIR's shyness, LORNA introduces her to FLORA.

LORNA
Mrs. Jean Briggs.

JEAN
Hello.

FLORA
Oh my goodness.

LORNA
This is my Auntie Flora.

FLORA
Alistair's my brother-in-law. He was married to my sister
Tina. We're sister-in-laws, you and me. No we're not.
Well nearly. You look very nice.

JEAN
Thank you.

FLORA
Alistair wanted to save his suit for church. We hope
you'll come with us to church tomorrow morning. The
whole county will want to meet you.

JEAN
Yes of course. Lorna was mentioning it to me.

LORNA
You don't go by Katie at all then?

JEAN
(*JEAN shakes her head.*) That was a long time ago. Your
dad of course, your dad called me Katie.

FLORA

Ewan and his dad will be along any second. We made a bedroom for him there in the parlour when he come home from the hospital. Ewan put in a shower. You got his chin.

JEAN

Pardon me?

FLORA

You got the same chin as Alistair, Mrs. Briggs.

JEAN

Please. Call me Jean.

FLORA

Jean. Would you like a cup of tea Jean?

JEAN

I'm fine.

FLORA

Or I've got ginger ale. Or diet cola. I'm trying to get Ewan interested in the diet soft drinks. It's a hard sell.

EWAN enters.

EWAN

She's trying to kill me with aspartame. One of her long range plans.

LORNA

This is my brother Ewan.

JEAN

Lorna's told me so much about you.

EWAN

Don't believe everything you hear.

FLORA

Where's your dad?

EWAN

He's coming.

LORNA

You sure?

EWAN

I'm sure.

FLORA

You'll want to be on your own with him I suppose?

JEAN

I don't know.

FLORA

You set the pace. Alistair, he's got no skill with that sort of thing.

LORNA

You let us know what you need.

JEAN

Thank you. Forgive me. I'm a little nervous.

LORNA

We all are. We're so happy you're here.

FLORA

(*to EWAN*) Go move that awful horse from the front field! No one wants to look at that when we're eating supper.

> *ALISTAIR enters, he walks with a cane, with difficulty. He doesn't look directly at JEAN.*

ALISTAIR
Good day then.

*ALISTAIR and JEAN shake hands. JEAN touches her
brother's shoulder tentatively, ALISTAIR remains stiff.*

ALISTAIR
You come on the train?

JEAN
No, no. I came on the airplane. Lorna picked me up in
Montreal.

FLORA
Was the plane on time?

JEAN
It was.

FLORA
Now there's a cause for celebration. Used to be that—

ALISTAIR
Stop talking Flora.

LORNA
Why don't we give you two some privacy.

ALISTAIR
Stay put. Everyone just stay put.

FLORA
(*pause*) Can I talk then?

ALISTAIR
Ah Jesus.

EWAN
(*pause*) You live on Vancouver Island Mrs. Briggs. That's
a great part of the world.

FLORA
Call her Jean.

JEAN
Comox.

FLORA
Near Victoria.

JEAN
Not really.

FLORA
A lot of English folk down there in Victoria. Double-decker buses.

JEAN
I don't really know Victoria very well. We lived in Chilliwack, on the mainland, for forty-two years. That's where we raised our girls.

ALISTAIR
You see them Chinese? Out there in the water?

JEAN
Pardon me?

ALISTAIR
Trying to swim their way into the country. Out there in B.C.

LORNA
The migrants from China who came on the boats last summer.

JEAN
Yes, yes. We donated a box of clothes.

ALISTAIR

I had a China man next door there, one bed over. He didn't like them swimmers one little bit ... You seen the storm on the box? She had to do all her cooking on the wood stove. Just like the old days.

LORNA

I think Dad's talking about the ice storm a couple of years ago. Ewan works for highways. He was a bit of a local hero. They had no power here for twenty-three days.

ALISTAIR

You got a wood stove?

JEAN

No.

ALISTAIR

We always got a back up system in place with the wood.

JEAN

I live in a condominium. There are rules about heating. Rules about everything.

ALISTAIR

That's what they need in the hospitals. Wood heat. People come out of there drug addicts, hooked on sleeping pills. I had a stroke.

JEAN

You look well.

ALISTAIR

Tina read in the paper there, the first lady doctor come out of McGill, the university there in Montreal. She

come over on the boats too. She come on the child
boats.

JEAN
I was a nurse. I trained at St. Joseph's in Montreal.

FLORA
Is that a Catholic institution?

JEAN
All the hospitals were Catholic then. But I was raised
United Church. My father was a minister. And my
mother, of course, a minister's wife. We had a busy
house.

FLORA
Very kind people, taking you in.

JEAN
They were just my parents. I didn't think of it that way.
But they were good people.

FLORA
Sure.

JEAN
We lived in Montreal, then in Sherbrooke. My husband
and I moved to B.C. when we got married.

ALISTAIR
He dead then?

JEAN
In 1993, heart disease.

LORNA
I'm sorry.

FLORA

Yes. I've got to turn down the potatoes.

JEAN

I hope you didn't go to too much trouble.

EWAN

She's been cooking since Tuesday.

FLORA

I haven't done a thing. Dorrie's bringing dessert—pie.
They've got lovely apples next door there. Ewan's darn
horse ate up our whole orchard.

EWAN

Wasn't me left the gate open.

*FLORA exits, her absence bringing about another awkward
pause.*

LORNA

Do you remember much Jean? From when you were
little?

JEAN

I remember the boat. It was awful. Everyone was sick.
And the big house in Montreal where I first stayed. I
thought it was a castle. We drove by there with our girls
in 1967. When we went to Expo.

ALISTAIR

We went to the fair in 1968 when the prices come down.

EWAN

When there was nothing left to see.

JEAN

I'm afraid I don't remember Scotland at all.

> *JEAN manages to make eye contact with ALISTAIR for the first time, he can't bear it.*

JEAN

Except for my brother. I remembered him. I always remembered my brother.

> *ALISTAIR stands up, heads off determinedly.*

EWAN

Where you off to?

LORNA

Dad—come sit back down.

ALISTAIR

I got to lie down. Get her to call me for supper.

> *ALISTAIR exits, another pause.*

EWAN

He gets wore out 'cause of the stroke.

JEAN

I hope I didn't offend him.

LORNA

Believe me—you're not the one who should be worried right now about being offensive.

JEAN

I didn't think I'd know his face today. But as soon as I saw him I knew it, clear as day.

> *LORNA takes JEAN's hand.*

JEAN

What I remember most is waiting.

LORNA

He won't talk to us about any of this. He won't talk to us
about anything.

JEAN

After a while I didn't know who I was waiting for
anymore. But I was still waiting.

Scene Six

Later that afternoon, lights up on DORRIE, on the porch.
She is cleaning out her purse, balling up old tissues.
WESLEY enters carrying two pies.

WESLEY

Why aren't you going in?

DORRIE

I can't go to supper with a handbag full of old Kleenex.
What would Mrs. Briggs think of that?

WESLEY

It'd be a shock all right ... C'mon now Mum. Flora'll
send in the army if we're late. She's been talking about
this supper for two months.

DORRIE

It's a special day.

WESLEY

Yes it is.

DORRIE

I keep thinking of that bald fellow we met at the
reunion. The one who went back to England with those
free plane tickets from the Aid. Fred.

WESLEY

All he found was some old cousin who'd never heard a'
him.

DORRIE

But they had the same hands. Big and bony. And wasn't
he proud—poor Fred.

WESLEY
He was indeed.

DORRIE
Tickled pink about those hands ... I suppose you'll be
happy to see Lorna. (*beat*) She'll be happy to see you
too.

WESLEY
Why don't we get her to move up here, give me a hand
with the milking.

DORRIE
You're making fun of me.

WESLEY
Let's go.

DORRIE
If the Aid had given us a plane ticket earlier I might
have gone back. See if anyone was left. See if there were
any there who looked like me.

WESLEY
Close up your purse now.

DORRIE
This handbag is thirty-five years old.

WESLEY
Mum. No one's gonna' notice.

DORRIE
If I'd got that letter when I first come I would've gone
right back on the first boat. Found my own little sister
before she passed away.

WESLEY helps DORRIE to the door.

WESLEY
You wanna' know who you look like? Me and Willie.

DORRIE
That isn't true. You boys are all your dad.

WESLEY
Dougie and Robert too. And twenty-two grandchildren and four great-grandchildren to boot.

Scene Seven

A couple of hours later—FLORA, DORRIE, WESLEY, JEAN,
LORNA, ALISTAIR and EWAN are gathered round the
table, finishing their dessert. DORRIE is part way through
a story.

DORRIE

> I was in Hazelbrae House in Peterborough when I first
> come. It was full of girls, waiting to go out working. Not
> many got adopted. But we'd miss the ones that did. I
> guess we were missing our own sisters, big and little.

JEAN

> When my parents came to pick me up my mother was
> wearing a fox stole. I thought it was made out of dog fur.
> My mother told me I didn't want to go with them. I
> cried and I screamed. I wanted to stay put.

DORRIE

> One lady who'd come to take home a little girl—you
> know what she done? She'd knit a pair of mitts for
> everyone of us girls who was left there at Hazelbrae. She
> told each and every one of us that we were very special
> girls. I'd never heard nothing like that before. I'd never
> heard nothing like that in my life.

FLORA

> Our homeboy Charlie—he come right from the streets
> of London. Me and Teeny, we'd fall over each other
> laughing every time he'd open his mouth. We thought
> Charlie talked like someone just come from the moon.

WESLEY

You hear that Mum? You're being compared to a creature from outer space.

FLORA

I didn't mean you Dorrie! I didn't think.

DORRIE

No one listen to Wesley. It was harder for the boys. Wasn't it Alistair? (*beat*) I got to work inside of course, in the house. Only time I had to go out was to bring in the wood. Bring in the water. That was my first job every morning. Starting up the fire. I was scared to death of that stove. Scared I wouldn't get it going right. Then when I did get it going I was sure I was going to burn the house down with everyone in it.

WESLEY

First up and last to bed every day. Eleven years old.

DORRIE

Well Mrs. McNab was up right after me.

WESLEY

Would've made a hen feel more welcome—

DORRIE

She had her hands full—all those children. I helped with the little ones. I liked that.

WESLEY

You're looking tired Mum.

DORRIE

Just a little.

WESLEY and DORRIE shake hands with JEAN.

WESLEY
It was a great pleasure for both of us Mrs. Briggs.

DORRIE
It was.

WESLEY
To be invited here on this special day.

LORNA
It's a day we'll never forget.

EWAN
That it is.

LORNA
Right, Dad?

ALISTAIR
Eh?

JEAN
(*pause*) It was a special day for me too. Thank you,
Flora—that was a wonderful meal.

LORNA
She looks after us all, Auntie Flora

> *LORNA and EWAN usher DORRIE and WESLEY out the
> door. FLORA clears away dishes.*

> *ALISTAIR and JEAN are left alone for the first time all
> day. ALISTAIR is shy, he moves from the table to the couch,
> JEAN follows him, sits beside him, she unwraps white tissue
> from a photograph very carefully.*

JEAN
There she is.

ALISTAIR
Eh?

JEAN
That's our mother.

ALISTAIR can't look.

ALISTAIR
Go ask Flora for the magnifying glass. She's got it in the
pantry, she's got a big drawer a' junk.

*JEAN leaves the photograph on the couch beside ALISTAIR,
she exits.*

*ALISTAIR sits still for a moment, then cautiously he
touches the tin frame around the photograph. LORNA
enters, he pulls his hand back quickly, as though caught.*

JEAN enters, hands ALISTAIR the magnifying glass.

LORNA
What's that?

JEAN
A picture of our mother.

ALISTAIR barely looks at the photograph.

ALISTAIR
That's her all right.

LORNA studies the photograph.

LORNA
She's so young ... So serious. She's beautiful Dad.

*JEAN unwraps another little packet, covered in the same
white tissue.*

JEAN
This was wrapped up along with the picture. A button, chipped, made out of bone. And a couple of little cotton dresses and four pairs of little wool gloves. That was all I brought with me from Scotland. In a tin trunk. I'd appreciate it Alistair—anything you could tell me about our mother.

ALISTAIR
Very fond of you, Mummy ...

LORNA
(*pause*) That's it?

ALISTAIR stands, he is hearing something the others can't hear. It is KATIE on the porch, he walks toward her, standing in the doorway, caught between past and present.

LORNA
Dad come sit down.

KATIE
Jackie ...

ALISTAIR goes back in time, he is on the porch, looking for KATIE, she hides.

ALISTAIR
Where the hell you got to now?

KATIE
SSsssh! SSsssh! SSsssh! I'm hiding from Mummy.

ALISTAIR
You let Mummy rest now. Hear?

KATIE
She no' a good hider, Mummy.

ALISTAIR
Get out from there.

KATIE
She just pulls the sheet over her head. An idiot'd know
that's still Mummy.

ALISTAIR
Come look what I got right here.

*ALISTAIR holds something in his hand. KATIE wiggles out
from under because she is desperate to see.*

KATIE
What is it?

ALISTAIR
Tuppence.

KATIE
That a lot?

ALISTAIR
Aye, t'is. She wants us to go to the shops.

KATIE
That for bread then?

ALISTAIR
No sir.

KATIE
Coal?

ALISTAIR
It's for anything we choose.

KATIE
Sweets Jackie?

ALISTAIR

Aye …

KATIE

How many? How many sweets?

ALISTAIR

Hurry up now. Put on your shoes.

KATIE is on the floor, buckling her shoes. ALISTAIR returns to the present, he looks toward JEAN.

ALISTAIR

She loved little Katie. Mummy loved her wee girl.

LORNA takes her dad's hand.

LORNA

Come back inside Dad.

ALISTAIR

She went to heaven from coughing, Mummy did.

JEAN

That isn't right

LORNA

Tuberculosis. T.B. probably—

ALISTAIR

That's it all right. That's what she had. So they shipped us off to Canada.

JEAN

She didn't die from tuberculosis.

ALISTAIR

You'll want to get back on the highway. You'll want to be on your way before it gets dark.

118

LORNA
Dad—

JEAN
I know how our mother died. I have papers from the
Children's Homes, from Barnardo's. A file of papers to
tell me about my mother's life. But I was so little, I can't
remember—

ALISTAIR
Not everything someone done is worth remembering.
Ever think of that?

JEAN
She'd no husband. She'd no help—

ALISTAIR
I helped.

JEAN
Our mother had no idea, none, what would happen to
you and me. To so many children. Nobody did. She
must've thought the way everybody did—there was a
chance for a good life for us in Canada. So she made a
decision.

ALISTAIR
You got that right. She made her choice.

LORNA
She gave you up. Dad? Is that right?

JEAN
She gave us up. And it broke her heart.

LORNA
Daddy?

ALISTAIR

> Leaving us all alone there for four days. We could 'a died right there. Nothing to eat but a wee bag of candy—

JEAN

> She'd a terrible life. Don't you dare suggest she didn't suffer. Forty years in an institution. She died all by herself in a hospital in Glasgow.

> *ALISTAIR freezes.*

ALISTAIR

> Eh?

LORNA

> Did you know that Daddy?

JEAN

> My daughter, she struggles with depression too.

ALISTAIR

> She sit in her bed all day then your daughter?

JEAN

> Sometimes, yes.

ALISTAIR

> She sign over her children to the Aid?

> *ALISTAIR starts to exit, he freezes at the porch.*

JEAN

> My daughter doesn't have any children. My daughter doesn't believe she deserves good things.

> *ALISTAIR goes back in time, he sees KATIE.*

KATIE
    Jackie ... Mummy's hiding. Jackie! Her bureau's empty!
    Her big coat's gone too ...

LORNA
    He'll go hide out in the barn. That's how he handles
    things he doesn't know how to handle. I'm sorry.

    JEAN begins to remember.

KATIE
    Mummy's gone.

JEAN
    A wee bag of candy ...

LORNA
    What's that?

KATIE
    She's gone Jackie ...

JEAN
    Two peppermints and a toffee for supper ... We came
    back from the store. Me and Jackie ... She was gone.

ALISTAIR
    (*to KATIE*) You come sit with me.

JEAN
    Your dad was in charge of the candy. For four days. Two
    peppermints and a toffee for breakfast and supper. Cold
    tea.

    ALISTAIR holds KATIE.

JEAN
    All for me. None for Jackie.

Scene Eight

*A few moments later, lights up on ALISTAIR, twilight. He
has stopped midway between the house and field, he's
exhausted. EWAN enters.*

ALISTAIR

You seen my big cat? She'll want a drink of milk. You go
get it.

EWAN

No.

ALISTAIR

It's no good for a boy cat, milk—

EWAN

Dad if Lorna disappeared off the face of the earth for
seventy years I hope I'd be at least relieved to see her.
Lorna wants us back inside. Now.

ALISTAIR

I go back in once that Jean's gone to her hotel there in
Cornwall.

EWAN

Oh for God's sake.

ALISTAIR

She's old as the hills, that Jean eh? She's a sight. And I'll
tell you something else. She's no relation to me.

EWAN

That isn't right Dad. She's your sister.

ALISTAIR

No sir.

EWAN
And she just came across the whole country to see you.

ALISTAIR
That old thing? I wouldn't 'a let her on the plane.
That's no' Katie.

EWAN
It is. And you damn well know it ... You've got to go
back in.

ALISTAIR
Can't do that. No sir.

EWAN
Lorna's gonna give us both shit if we don't go.

ALISTAIR
You go tell her. You go tell that Jean, that as soon as I
found out where she was, I tried to come see her. I tried
to come twice. I got in some trouble there Ewan. Got in
some trouble at that first farm I come to. Eighteen
months in that jail ...

EWAN
You went to jail?

ALISTAIR
That jail for boys in Uxbridge.

*LORNA and JEAN listen from the porch, ALISTAIR doesn't
know they are there.*

ALISTAIR
You tell that Jean I tried to walk there to Montreal. Sixty-
two miles to Montreal. I made it to Vankleek Hill then I
had to turn round to be back at work the next day. So I

done extra work for four months then I had enough for a train.

I went to that big place there. I went to the Aid. A lady there, she was nice to me. She told me my sister had been adopted and that I wasn't to see her. She had a new life. She told me she knew the ones who took my sister in personal. That they were dandy folk. Just as nice as could be. That's what she told me. So I took the train back.

EWAN

And that was that. Case closed.

ALISTAIR

I walked into the barn. Killed two cows, milkers. Shot dead—boom boom. Woulda' killed more but that farmer come. Then the mounted police.

EWAN

Jesus Dad.

ALISTAIR

That's not right, killing cows for no good reason. My dad there in Edinburgh—he done things like that. He done things like that everyday a' the week.

EWAN

You could've told us. You didn't have to hide everything.

ALISTAIR sees JEAN and LORNA.

ALISTAIR

Soon as I come outta' that place in Uxbridge I gone right back there to Montreal. Second time there? That lady at the Aid wasn't so nice. She'd had it up to here with boys like me. And I didn't like her one little bit either. But she had a point.

Katie's gonna get on a whole lot better without the likes of me. She's gotta' give her new mummy and daddy a chance. I started using MacEachern, that was our granny's name. I never liked my real name 'cause it was the same as my dad's—Alistair Jackman—but they always called him Jack and I was little Jackie. Best thing that ever happened to you was that he was out the door before you was born. I use MacEachern so you won't run away to find me. I come here. I worked there at MacIlwane's. I was a big boy by then. I was fourteen.

JEAN joins ALISTAIR.

JEAN
She was wrong. The lady at the Aid. I didn't get on better without you. I waited Jackie. I waited and I waited.

ALISTAIR
I kept thinking you'd find me anyway. Come running through the hay, over there, from the east. It didn't make sense, that kind of thinking. It was a silly thing …

JEAN
I loved you. You were my brother.

ALISTAIR
(*pause*) I'm still your brother … It was me give you that little button.

Not much of a present. One little button that's broke.

JEAN
It was everything.

JEAN and ALISTAIR walk slowly toward KATIE, she is looking out, pointing.

KATIE

Jackie, there's a motor car! Right out front ...

ALISTAIR

You'd been at that window for four days.

KATIE

And a man. Got a little suit, little bow tie too.

ALISTAIR

The man there ... The man will want us to go with him.

KATIE

Take us to Mummy?

ALISTAIR

I don't know where it is we're going.

KATIE

What if Mummy comes back and we're no' here?

JEAN

There was a nosey old lady who lived below us.

KATIE

Mrs. Fergus! She'll keep an eye out for Mummy.

JEAN

His suit was blue, the man that came and took us. And I said—

KATIE

I don't want to go.

KATIE plops herself down defiantly on the ground at JEAN and ALISTAIR's feet, she turns her back to them.

JEAN
  I didn't want to go. So you told me—

ALISTAIR
  Are you daft then?

KATIE and JEAN
  I won't go.

ALISTAIR
  You really no' want to go in a motor car?

KATIE
  Jackie! We go in the motor car?

JEAN
  You told me I could sit in the front.

KATIE
  No! I want to sit in the back!

ALISTAIR
  I'll sit in the front then.

KATIE
  No!

ALISTAIR
  It doesn't matter a good god damn where we sit.

KATIE
  I want to sit beside you. Sit beside you all the way.

  *KATIE starts to back away from ALISTAIR. ALISTAIR
  turns to JEAN.*

ALISTAIR
  She'd red hair Mummy. She worked in a glove factory.
  She liked her tea without sugar. She'd give her sugar to
  you and me. She wouldn't sing the hymns in church

because she thought her voice would spoil the service.
She was funny.

JEAN

The car was cold. It smelled of boots.

ALISTAIR

It was raining.

JEAN

I'm kneeling, looking out. You're beside me Jackie.

ALISTAIR

Of course I am.

JEAN

I'm looking for her big coat. Forever. I'm looking for
Mummy.

ALISTAIR

You sit back down now, proper.

KATIE

Jackie? Where are we?

ALISTAIR

I don't know.

Alistair looks toward KATIE one last time.

KATIE

Bundle me up Jackie. Bundle me up.

ALISTAIR

Aye. I'm right here. Katie—

End of play.